WHATEVER HAPPENED TO . . . ?

The Ultimate Sequels Book

ADRIAN MOURBY

Illustrated by Graham Round

SOUVENIR PRESS

First published 1997 by
Souvenir Press Ltd,
43 Great Russell Street, London WC1B 3PA
and simultaneously in Canada

Reprinted 1997

ISBN 0 285 63401 1

Typeset by Rowland Phototypesetting Ltd,
Bury St Edmunds, Suffolk
Printed in Great Britain by
Redwood Books, Trowbridge, Wiltshire

To Brian King

a very rare kind of BBC producer

who saw a series

in what I thought was just a funny idea

CONTENTS

Whatever Happened To . . .
PINOCCHIO?

These days it really isn't easy being a fairy. We all go into the job because we like granting dearest wishes to good little children, but there's just so much red tape to get through nowadays! Even after Pinocchio had saved Gepetto from the Monsters of the Deep, and heroically assisted him in all his infirmities, it still took eight months to process his application through normal channels. Then we got held up at the European Court of Human Rights (Admissions Section). At last, however, I was able to grant Pinocchio's dearest wish and turn him into a Real Boy. Mind you, if I'd known how things were going to fall out I don't think I'd have bothered.

The problem was definitely in the aftercare. At the time of his transformation into a human being you couldn't have imagined a nicer child than Pinocchio, nor a more doting father than Gepetto. Unfortunately I had no choice but to leave the two of them to get on with it in the hope that they would live happily ever after. It was unrealistic, I know, but we fairies don't have the resources to do much else. Really, what Pinocchio needed at this time was counselling to prepare him for human existence. He had *such a lot* of new experiences to get used to.

If you think about it, this poor child had never even been to the lavatory before. Having been carved out of a log, Pinocchio had no experience whatsoever of the human digestive tract. Imagine the shock of excreting for the first time at the age of ten!

And then physical pain, that was a problem too. Little Pinocchio had always liked to pretend he was hard. A lot of boys do but it's so much easier when you're made of cherry wood. He used to encourage other children to hammer nails into his nose. When that had to stop I think he felt a certain loss of face.

But the real problem was his father. Gepetto Polendina was not really suited to rearing an adolescent. My colleagues in the Social Services take the view that Pinocchio had been completely beyond the discipline of his foster-father from the start. While the boy was still a puppet he had failed to prevent him running away to join a fairground, and then, when Pinocchio needed a father figure most, what did Gepetto do? He got himself swallowed by a giant shark and spent a few months at the bottom of the sea.

There was a brief, *pre*pubescent, honeymoon period when all seemed well, but within a year we had a rebellious teenager on our hands. Gepetto Polendina was a very old man and a bachelor. He wanted Pinocchio to stay a little boy. He certainly had no idea how to cope once the sap started rising. As for Pinocchio . . . well, if defecating was quite a shock to him, imagine the effect of pubic hair and testosterone. I'm sure these experiences must have made the child wholly disenchanted with his new life as a Real Boy.

The two of them used to argue a lot, often over silly things. This is quite normal when there are teenagers in the family, but I know it really hurt Gepetto when Pinocchio took to boycotting wood products. He would say to me, '*How does Dad know that piece of wood wants to be a table leg more than a cricket bat? He never even bothers to ask!*' That may sound extreme, but I can see how disturbing it must be if one's foster-father spends his days chopping lumps off one's nearest relatives. Poor Gepetto simply didn't understand. He said to me, '*Good Fairy, how can I ever talk to him? He shouts and shouts and then storms out and slams the door. He never tells me where he's going. He'll tell the door but he won't tell me.*'

My colleagues in the Social Services say it's obvious in retrospect that we should have assessed Gepetto far more stringently before allowing him to foster Pinocchio. Normally we try to match ethnic background, but Pinocchio and Gepetto weren't even the same species!

In his teens young Pinocchio proved easy picking for extremist political groups. On his thirteenth birthday he joined the provisional wing of Friends of the Earth. On one occasion he and several former Bavarian

Nutcrackers broke down fences around the Forestry Commission land and daubed slogans condemning the forced breeding of trees in captivity. Another time they smashed the windows of an Aga showroom. This led to Pinocchio's first arrest. As the fairy assigned to this particular family I was called in and tried to persuade Pinocchio to apologise for damaging the wood-burning stoves, or 'death camps' as he would insist on terming them. But when Pinocchio came up before the magistrates he was rude and abusive and used the court case to draw attention to his campaign for nuclear power which he claimed to be a much safer form of fuel, at least as far as trees were concerned.

Pinocchio was given three months community service during which time he absconded and led a vicious revenge attack on a well-known french polisher. The poor man was sanded down and buffed with a power tool before the police arrived. Released on bail, Pinocchio told me he felt that all his life he had been misled by 'anthropomorphic cultural imperialism'. He claimed that everyone, even the Fox and Cat, had deceived him into believing there was something inherently good about being human and that he was now suffering alienation. '*I'm only trying to get back to my roots*,' he explained.

Eventually I was required to serve formal notice that if Pinocchio Polendina did not make a more determined effort to fit into society he would be turned back into a block of cherry wood. Pinocchio replied that for him

compliance would go completely against the grain. *'What's so great about being human?'* he insisted. *'You don't get trees fouling up the ozone layer and crapping everywhere. But look at how humans treat us in return: they grow us in battery conditions, chop us down, pine-strip us into cheeseboards and then burn us. What have we ever done to hurt them, except lose our footing and squash a few lumberjacks?'* He was unpersuadable. *'We'll all be dead one day!'* he shouted. *'I'll just be so much dead wood.'*

According to UNWIT (United Nations World Initiative for Trees), this country has a particularly harsh Vegetable Rights Record. I'm sorry to say that last month the authorities carried out their threat and Pinocchio was turned back into a wooden puppet. It was some consolation to me that we were able to get him into a nice little private toy shop. When I left him there I warned that he'd have to get used to someone else pulling the strings from now on. *'We're all manipulated,'* he explained to me. Defiant to the end.

I must say that I do feel a failure. We good fairies have such limited powers. I wish we could wave a magic wand and put everything right, but life just isn't like that. Mind you, it has to be said that the main responsibility lies firmly with Gepetto. In my opinion the man should never have been allowed to carve himself a son in the first place.

The Social Services go further. They say he should be strung up.

Whatever Happened To . . .
FRANKENSTEIN'S MONSTER?

From *The Unpublished Casebook of Sigmund Freud*

At the beginning of the Summer of 1913 I placed an advert in the tobacconist's window on the corner of Tiefengriefenstrasse. *Good Jewish doctor seeks non-Jewish neurotics for purposes of comparative study*, the card read. My portfolio of meshugem and psychos was now very full but I needed a few goyem to balance out my findings and, oh boy, did I find some. The best, without a doubt, was a seven-foot-tall neurotic with skin problems who worked as a wick-trimmer on the Fahrtgasseplatz. I shall call this patient the *Self-made Man*, although he clung persistently to the fiction that the person who had actually created him was one Viktor Frankenstein of Ulm.

'You mean to tell me that you were brought to life from inanimate tissue?' I exclaimed in disbelief.

'In a lightning storm,' he added.

'A lightning storm!' I replied (I tell you there's *nothing* I haven't heard in my job).

I had hoped to probe the patient's history and, over several sessions, draw out the tangled web of his inner anxieties but, believe me, with this boy there was no holding back. 'Frankenstein, whom I detest above all others, fashioned me for his own vanity, despaired when he looked upon my hideousness and refused to form for me a mate. Seeing that I was doomed to live this life in the bitterest of isolation I revenged myself on my creator by destroying Elisabeth, his betrothed—and various other people who came to hand. I then took flight into the icy wastes where I lived, in misery, for seventy long and desolate years.'

I tell you, don't let anyone ever say these Gentiles don't know how to screw up! Unfortunately my Gabelsberger shorthand wasn't fast enough to keep up with all this kibitzing and all the pacing to and fro, but I had to stop him anyway. He was a big boy, this *Self-made Man*, and Mrs Rosenbaum from the flat down below, she came up and hammered on the door. 'Don't worry, Mrs Rosenbaum,' I said. 'It's just one of my neurotics. Isn't the weather a lot better today!'

So, what did I do? I made us both some Vompfongler's Herbal Tea, then I suggested that together he and I might analyse what I'd heard so far.

'What d'you mean *analyse*?' he asked.

'He wants to know what I mean!' I replied. 'Listen, my boy, from the moment you came in through that door I could see that here was a walking, 22-carat case of father hatred, probably the result of having accidentally witnessed, as a child, your parents making love.'

'But I didn't—' he interjected.

'Blotted out,' I explained with a wave of my Winkel-moos Patent Propelling Pencil. 'Don't worry about it. Listen to me, Vienna is absolutely full of people trauma-tised by having witnessed, as a child, their parents making love. I meet them everywhere and the interest-ing thing is: *each one of them* has blotted out the memory!'

What I didn't tell him was that it was clear to me that this boy's condition was allied to an unusually deep sense of personal inadequacy. Unusual? He should be so lucky. According to my patient, since 'escaping' from the Arctic wastes, some time around the end of the last century, this boy had lived without female companion-ship of any kind. (And before that there'd only been penguins.) During the early 1900s my *Self-made Man* had worked for a while on a small yoghurt farm in Sweden where no one took any notice of a neurotic seven-foot-tall goatherd with green skin who claimed to have been brought to life by a shaft of lightning (but then, as I said to Mrs Rosenbaum, you know what those Swedes are like).

Nevertheless, even the Scandinavians, who are nor-mally at it like David and Bathsheba, had drawn a line at my patient, and he clearly blamed this Viktor Frankenstein for his failure to find himself a girlfriend.

'So now,' I said. 'Let us try and see this dream of yours in symbolic form.'

'What do you mean *dream*?' he asked.

'He wants to know what I mean *dream*,' I replied. 'Listen, I tell you. Fantasising about violence towards the father figure is a traditional male response during, and even predating, adolescence. The young male child cannot accept that his mother finds another man more sexually desirable. Consequently this man becomes a figure of hatred for the young male who then jostles with him for a position of pre-eminence. Failing to seduce his mother from the father, the male child then looks to other women for solace, but in this act he still wishes for his father's approval. In your case this seeking after approval takes an extreme form because you claim you asked your father actually to *create* for you a mate. The refusal of the father to do this then led to an out-break of open father/son hostility which remains unre-solved in your poor sick mind. Here, have another bagel.'

'But Frankenstein was *not* my father,' the *Self-made Man* insisted. 'He was my sole creator, fashioning me out of inanimate skin, some nuts and bolts and a few pointy bits of his own devising. I was not born but reanimated in a thunderstorm.'

'Listen, my boy,' I told him. 'If you'd been reani-mated by a lightning rod you'd be so many pieces of burnt schnitzel by now.'

The *Self-made Man* was most emphatic that my interpretation of his claims was inaccurate.

'I had *no mother!*' he exclaimed, bursting into sobs.

'Everyone has a mother,' I reasoned with him. 'Some of us wish we didn't but there you go. You are simply denying yours because you believe she didn't love you enough. When you talk of *killing* this Elisabeth, this fiancée of Dr Frankenstein, what you are really speaking of is the fact that your mother was *dead to you* once you realised that your father used to *bumsen* with her every Saturday night. And when you speak of this Frankenstein pursuing you to the Arctic wastes, don't ask me to believe you really got on a ship and bought a one-way ticket, baggage class, to the North Pole! Of course not! You were speaking symbolically of a subsequent frigidity in your own relationships with girlies. Tell me, do you have a problem getting it up?'

At this point the creature seized me with preternatural strength and rained curses upon me for my sniggering schoolboy stupidity.

'As you are so far into denial,' I gasped, 'I would suggest we end this session here.'

Two days later the *Self-made Man* came to see me again. I had been expecting him, as I knew that once he had loosened his grip on my throat he would begin to see the inescapable logic of interpretive psychoanalysis. But it turned out that following an unfortunate incident in the Titsengraben, involving a prostitute who took all his money but refused to hold his hand, he was in need of the three schillings I was paying. I was sweeping the stairs with Mrs Rosenbaum when he arrived, which was unfortunate as the poor woman suddenly screamed and ran into her apartment screeching, 'Golem! Golem!'

'You see what I mean,' said the *Self-made Man*.

'Golem schmolem,' I told him, and suggested we went upstairs for some pretzels, but this boy was already in kibitzing mode and there was no stopping him now. On and on he went about how hideous he was, and how this was all the fault of that Frankenstein (the name which he insisted on using for his father). I was just trying to reload the old Winkelmoos when I realised that the *Self-made Man* was telling me something very important regarding what I had said about his long-term unresolved anger. He was concerned that there was no possibility for closure on this one, given the fact that Viktor Frankenstein had died in the middle of the last century.

'How old *are* you?' I asked, intrigued, because I tell you I was at that moment pondering a very interesting theory about the possibility of delayed adolescence.

'One hundred and forty-two,' he replied. Well, you win some, you lose some . . .

'Listen,' I said. 'Self-revulsion is an external focus for inner unhappiness. I have had beautiful girls in here, girls you could take home to meet your mother—if you had one, that is—girls who could bring a room full of rabbis to attention, and yet these girls were convinced of their own repulsiveness.'

'I have a *bolt* through my neck,' he growled at me.

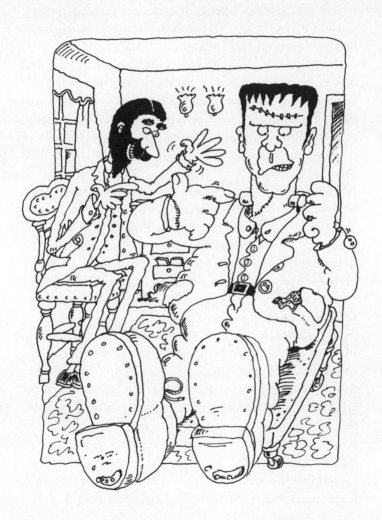

'He says he has a bolt through his neck!' I replied. 'Listen, if you had a *bolt* through your neck you would be unable to eat and breathe.'

'What is this, then?' he cried in some distress, loosening his collar stud and showing me what did indeed look very much like a bolted metal plate positioned to appear as if it were holding his head in place.

'Why have you done this to yourself?' I asked.

'I didn't do it!' he exclaimed. 'This is what *Frankenstein* did to me.'

'Remove it,' I commanded, putting down my Egon Schiel doodlepad and speaking in my very firmest voice.

'If I remove it my stupid head will fall off!' he cried. Patiently, but with great authority, I pointed out the huge symbolic importance of that bolt, and that *until he took it off* he would continue to suffer unresolved anger, huge bouts of revulsion and great difficulty getting girlfriends.

This failing, I gave him the works: a complete analysis of what he had disclosed to me so far. By mutilating himself in such a way the *Self-made Man* was hoping to make the hated father figure feel guilty; however, he was simultaneously tormented by his inability to achieve this, given that the 'Frankenstein' father was dead. The result was that in the end the only person he was hurting was himself.

'I am so hideous!' he cried. 'Little children run away from me, even that fat old Viennese tart on the stairs!'

22

'You are not hideous,' I argued. 'For someone of 142 you're really quite a looker. The problem lies in this deliberate self-mutilation. You do not feel yourself capable of being loved because your mother chose your father over you.'

'You think I want to have a bolt through my neck?' he shrieked at me.

'Take it off, then,' I commanded for a second time. 'You will feel much better.'

At this point the patient, incensed by the unanswerable logic of my argument, did indeed withdraw the bolt from his neck. To this day I regard that action as one of the greatest triumphs for interpretive psychoanalysis.

Unfortunately, two days later the poor man died when his head fell off. Nevertheless, I am proud to say that for those two days he was completely cured of all neuroses.

Whatever Happened To . . .
JANE EYRE?

Oh Reader, was I wrong to marry him?

When first Mr Rochester and I lived as man and wife he was as dependent on me as a newborn babe. The great conflagration at Thornfield had robbed my husband of his eyes, one of his hands and much of that manly spirit which had pulsed, for so long, below the fine buckle of his belt. Yet gradually the physicians restored to Mr Rochester his sight—just as I restored the roof to Thornfield and aided my husband in the recovery of those other 'faculties' he believed he had lost.

Reader, no woman was ever nearer her mate nor happier than I, when first I put our newborn child into his hand—*hands* I should have said, but that the artificial limb designed by Old John and myself still needed certain modifications.

Because I had so many things to occupy my time—running the estate, directing the architects and conferring with various prostheticians—dear Mr Rochester was as much nursemaid and mother to our young Phoebus as I in those early years.

But as his strength returned my husband grew dispu-
tatious, and envious of my mastery of Thornfield. He
even refused to bottle-feed our own dear boy, declaring
that the child should be despatched to a board school
as soon as possible. My own views on such institutions
ran very much to the contrary and, since my marriage,
I had become a fervent apostle of our new Queen and
her belief that the family should be reared at home.

'D--- you and your New Victorian values!' my husband would cry when I refused to be persuaded of his
plan, and he would seize a brand from the fireplace
before departing angrily into the night.

Dear reader, let me now confide to you that when
first I was governess at Thornfield I often saw Old John
in the morning removing some blackened table or chair
from the house. In my naïveté, I always assumed that
Mr Rochester and his friend Dr Carfax had, during
one of their late-night gentlemen's *soirées*, allowed some
coals to spill from the fender and thereby char the furniture. Consequently, I gave these sights little heed, nor
did I much attend the pails of water that older servants
in the house would leave out in the corridors of an
evening. Indeed, so *little* did I heed them that often I
would trip over a bucket or two on my way up or
down the stairs. However, once I had become mistress
of Thornfield I decided to remonstrate soundly with
Old John about the folly of keeping so much water
about the place.

'Ee, but Mrs Rochester,' he said. 'Tha never knows when God's good watter mayt coom in handy.' Which, at the time, I thought to be the usual kind of unintelligible, superstitious nonsense one can expect from these Yorkshire folk. How misguided, how terribly misguided, I was.

It was only in the months following Mr Rochester's recovery, when a number of his tenants had been made homeless by sudden night-time conflagrations, that my suspicions grew, alerted not by the unusually high incidence of combustion in our neighbourhood, nor by the fact that my husband would sit upon the roof of Thornfield and watch the cottages burn, but by his uncommon generosity to the tenantry so dispossessed. Instead of driving these improvident creatures from his estate my husband would often compensate them from his fob. Fool that I was, I even found this a curiously attractive aspect of my spouse's character until the occasion of dear Phoebus' fifth birthday. It was only when my husband presented our little son with his own inscribed silver tinderbox that I began to ponder the cause of these frequent blazes.

Could it be, I wondered, that the dreadful conflagration which had been the death of poor mad Bertha Rochester—and the cause of my husband's debilitating injuries—could it be that this fire had been deliberately started by my troubled spouse? And might this, in any way, have a relation to the fact that my soulmate's manly spirit only ever seemed to pulse within him when we eschewed the marriage bed and lay down together before a roaring fire? Reader, you will understand that although I paid little heed to my doubts I emulated our own dear Queen by ensuring that young Phoebus spent more time in the nursery playing with his moppets. I also fitted a lock of my own construction to the nursery door and strengthened the bars on every window, lest my husband try to gain access from his roof-top haunts.

As I have already related, it had occurred to me that Mr Rochester's dangerous behaviour and his violent outbursts might have their root in those problems which lay below the buckle of his belt. Having read our own dear Queen's monograph upon *the stiffening of manly resolve*, I applied to the Army & Navy Stores for a device that Her Majesty had found most efficacious in the production of so many royal children. Alas, as I was demonstrating the little traction engine and its bellows to Mr Rochester, he became angrier than I have ever known.

'I will have no more of your woman's interference!' he cried. 'And as for that boy, he spends too much time sitting there fiddling with his moppets! He will go to school forthwith!' Thus speaking, Mr Rochester strode out of the door, knocking over Old John and leaving him stone dead.

Such was the force of Mr Rochester's anger, and such my fear of what else his rage might lead him unto, that I actually prevailed upon Grace Poole, my husband's sinister minion, to run for Dr Carfax. As well as being a man of seeming good sense, Dr Carfax also sat on the board of our local asylum. Alas, how cruelly I was deceived in him, for the doctor took one look at Her Majesty's Patent Stiffening Engine and declared, 'Rochester, you are being tormented beyond all endurance!' Moreover, the doctor agreed with my husband that Phoebus should be removed from my influence forthwith. You may imagine my distress, dear reader, as I took flight to the nursery, my poor boy whimpering all the time and clutching pitifully at his moppets. Determinedly I threw every bolt, and only just in time, for my triumphant husband soon resorted to his customary mode of argument, kicking furiously at the doors and demanding that I hand over the boy. Having failed to reason with me thus, he resorted to the axe, with which he belaboured the portals, but he little knew that I had recently had each door reinforced with iron plates of my own design and he soon tired of the exertion.

Oh reader, Phoebus and I have been living in this attic for two weeks now. My husband, failing to move me by shouting through the splintered lintels, has posted his creature, Grace Poole, outside the nursery, but when she sleeps I descend to the scullery to seek out food for us. I know that Mr Rochester does not care what befalls me but he is determined that our boy should have a traditional English upbringing and spend less time with his family.

Last even, dear reader, I heard a dreadful splintering of furniture which at the time I little heeded. Such noises were never uncommon at Thornfield when it was too wet for Mr Rochester to venture out at night. Now, however, with the stable clock showing one in the morning, I have woken to the smell of smoke, and when I open the door I can see the staircase barred by broken tables and chairs. Reader, you may think me mad when I speak of these things, but I am sure that my husband is of a mind to smoke Phoebus and myself out of our refuge. And if we will not quit the nursery voluntarily, then I fear he will do for me, his wife, as he did for poor Bertha Rochester before me. I care not for my own life but only for that of my son whom I wish to see rescued from the flames and yet not rescued to be reared by a madman. Dear reader, should these few lines be found, I beg you, in the name of my child and of me, his mother, to send succour and rescue immediately to Thornfield.

Or, to put it another way, *HELP!*

Whatever Happened To . . .
THE BIG BAD WOLF?

House of Commons written reply

From: The Rt Hon the Home Secretary

To: The Hon Member for Dark Wood (Central)

Re: THE ALLEGEDLY BIG BAD WOLF

I thank the Honourable Member for giving me this opportunity to put on record my high regard for members of the British Wolf Community who have made a considerable contribution to our culture. I'm also grateful for this opportunity to commend the work of our police force in their superlative handling of what has been a very sensitive inquiry.

The Honourable Member for Dark Wood (Central) has asked if I would agree with her that *throughout the investigation into the Pig, Riding-Hood and Duck attacks, Central Dark Wood Police systematically victimised members of the Wolf community*. I would reply that, on the contrary, they did everything in their power to ensure that no wolf was ever unfairly accused of gobbling up another species.

Turning to the first spate of incidents which became known in the press as 'The Little Pig Murders', I would point out that, although much tabloid attention was devoted to the reports of huffing and puffing in the vicinity of those houses where the first two attacks occurred, the police consistently *refused* to be influenced by the age-old prejudice that this is a chosen method of gaining illegal entry amongst the Wolf community.

If I may come now to the attempted gobbling up of a third little pig on 15th March this year: I am glad to say that Dark Wood's officers rightly refused to assume a connection between this assault and the previous two. True, all three victims were members of the same family (*non-ruminant omnivorous ungulate bristly Suidae*) and, in terms of height, all three could accurately be described as *of below average stature*, but the police did draw crucial distinctions between the first little pig who had built his house of straw, the second who had built his house of sticks, and the third whose dwelling was of timber-framed, breeze-block and brick construction. It was the press, *not the police*, who jumped to the conclusion that a serial killer was at large.

In reaction to these scaremongering tactics the Chief Constable of Dark Wood quite rightly called a media briefing (26th March) and made it unequivocally clear that there was no firm evidence linking these killings to the Wolf community. He appealed for Lupine leaders everywhere to cooperate in eliminating the possibility of wolf involvement.

Unfortunately a great deal of credence was given in the media to the third little pig's claim that a Big Bad Wolf had been on his roof trying to get down the chimney *because* he had failed to gain access by huffing and puffing. In my opinion the press behaved in a thoroughly irresponsible manner on this occasion, applauding the little pig for taking matters into his own trotters and commending him for heating a cauldron of water in the fireplace below. As I have frequently stated, we simply cannot have our citizens boiling unknown intruders in that manner. When officers arrested the third little pig for possession of an offensive weapon (*to wit: the cauldron*), there was an outcry in the press who seemed to be far more interested in tracking down the felon who had been on Mr Pig's roof at the time.

On 1st April, contrary to strict Home Office guidelines, a member of the *mainly*-Wolf community was arrested following a fresh assault in the Dark Wood constituency.

The suspect Mr B. B. Wolf, had been detained in a citizen's arrest by a Mr Riding-Hood, father of the alleged victim. Miss Riding-Hood claimed that on calling at her grandmother's house she had found Mr Wolf dressed in her grandmother's clothes and that he had tried to eat her. Subsequently she had discovered her relative tied up and locked in a cupboard.

There was of course a perfectly reasonable explanation for these events which Mr Wolf disclosed once he had consulted with his solicitor. It seems that for some years he had been enjoying what we might describe as an 'adult' relationship with Granny, which involved sexual practices of a dangerous nature. Mr Wolf would have released Granny in plenty of time to stop her asphyxiating had not little Red Riding-Hood burst in, followed by her father with his axe.

The police took the view, rightly in my opinion, that the unfortunate suffocation of Granny in the cupboard during the ensuing struggle was entirely the fault of her son-in-law. A decision was taken not to press charges of manslaughter against Mr B. B. Wolf. However, Mr Blue Riding-Hood, an Australian of belligerent temper, was arrested for carrying an offensive weapon and the Chief Constable called another press conference to assert that an axe was a dangerous instrument in anyone's hands.

Following the release of Mr Wolf, substantial police efforts went into trying to assuage the public's fears, rebuilding relations with the *mainly*-Wolf community and suppressing a series of protests by female activists who were calling for the castration of all canines.

I myself took the unprecedented step at this time of appearing on television and warning against giving a dog a bad name.

Two weeks later, on 14th April, there were strong

and legitimate protests from the *mainly*-Wolf community when Mr B. B. Wolf was once again apprehen-
ded while going about his lawful business. On this
occasion the citizen's arrest was performed by some
Jolly Huntsmen, acting on the eye-witness account of
a boy named Peter who claimed that he had observed
Mr Wolf in the act of gobbling up an entire duck. The
boy, Peter, lived with his grandfather in the Deep Forest
area of Central Dark Wood and admitted that he had
been spying on passers-by from a tall, tall tree when he
claimed to have seen Mr Wolf eating the duck in such
haste that the poor creature was swallowed in one gulp.
This preposterous story, from a self-confessed voyeur,
was nevertheless lent some credibility by veterinarians
who asserted that they could hear the bird actually singing inside the wolf's stomach.

One again Mr Wolf was able to give a completely
plausible explanation, as soon as he had spoken to his
solicitor. It seems that this blameless creature had not
been eating the bird in question but kissing her in an
intimate manner, their friendship being of a long and
passionate nature. There has been much tabloid derision
of this explanation, but I for one find it perfectly reasonable that, on realising that he was being observed from
a tree by the child, Peter, the shocked wolf gulped and,
accidentally, swallowed the duck whole. I myself, while
electioneering, had a very similar experience when a
flash-gun went off while I was kissing a baby, and I

have no difficulty whatsoever in believing Mr Wolf's account.

It should be noted that Mr Wolf was at great pains to cooperate with the police and even offered to have his stomach pumped if the duck might be saved. Unfortunately it subsequently emerged that she had drowned in the orange sauce that Mr Wolf had also consumed.

I would like to point out that following protests from Lupine community elders and the Royal Society for the Prevention of Cruelty to Animal Minorities, I, as Home Secretary, have joined in criticism of the boy, Peter, for trapping Mr Wolf in a noose from his vantage point in the tall, tall tree. Not only was this inhumane, it made it impossible for Mr Wolf immediately to regurgitate the bird as was, clearly, his wish. This government has refused to endorse newspaper claims that the child, Peter, is some kind of 'have-a-go hero'.

I am glad to say that the Dark Wood Constabulary have chosen not to press any charges against Mr Wolf who is clearly an upstanding member of his species and a credit to this country. Mr Wolf has now initiated a claim for damages against Peter, Mr Riding-Hood and the third little pig. I understand he is also threatening to take proceedings against the police for repeated wrongful arrest.

I would like to make it clear to the Honourable Member for Dark Wood (Central), and indeed to Mr Wolf himself, that our police officers did, on all possible occasions, bend over backwards to deflect suspicion and accusation away from members of the *mainly*-Wolf community. If they can bend any further I'm sure they will.

Whatever Happened To . . .
ROMEO?

Transcript of the Confession of *Rosaline Montague* as heard by one Friar Lawrence of Verona and never before published.

Forgive me, father, for my sins are grievous. But, between thee and me, I've never been of better cheer.

Not that I owe any thanks to you. Do you remember my last confession? How you told me that I should cease being prey to foul jealousy if only I could quit my brooding upon Juliet Capulet? Well I'm sorry, but I did try. I said all the *Ave Marias* you recommended. And a few more, and 'tis true I was feeling pretty goodly about myself. But as soon as I got home and saw Him descanting about the place, melancholy unnatural fat lump that he is, I just knew it had worked not. In fact, now I remember, methinks we can add the sin of Wrath to my list of transgressions. And Goblet-smashing, if that counts.

You see, over the past few weeks I've been going to Wise-counselling, and what I've come to realise is that the problem isn't with me. It's Romeo. I've tried putting the past behind us. I truly have. But what chance is there of that when the peevish toad is always descanting on about Her? *'Juliet wouldn't have minded if I left my doublet on the floor of our bedchamber. Juliet truly loved me.'* I beseech you, Friar, how can he *say* that? Juliet only spent one night with him—and she was thirteen at the time! People rate your favours more highly at that age. In any case I'm thirty-three. I need a *grown-up* husband. Oh, you wouldn't believe how green and immature he is. He thinks that if a woman doesn't plunge a dagger into her breast for him then she doesn't really care. Well I'm *sorry*, but there are limits to what I'll do to gain my husband's good opinion!

I tell you, there have been moments when I really wished you hadn't got that antidote to him in time. *If only!* I've thought. Had he but died in Capulet's tomb with Her, then perchance they could both be in Paradise together and he'd find out she wasn't so bloody marvellous after all.

I told him lots of men lose their wives. Old Martino's had three. It's an occupational hazard of producing an heir. Why *my* husband's first wife has to be so prized and perfect I simply cannot conjure. I knew Juliet Capulet, you know. Knew her for years. She was a wanton flirt, even at thirteen. And she had flat feet. She waddled. Like a duck.

Of course *he* didn't have time to notice *that*. And if he did, he's forgotten. Time's limping memory hath everyone deceived. She's become this perfect image of a teenage girl in love now, hasn't she? They strew statues to her all over Verona, but what nobody seems to remember is that he was going out with *me* at the time he met Her. It was to see *me* that he and Mercutio came to tickle the senseless rushes at that ball. We'd even arranged that he'd drop round to my balcony afterwards for some dalliance. But did he hell. He stood me up. On my own balcony, while he does dalliance elsewhere! Next thing I know Tybalt's killed Mercutio, Romeo's stabbed Tybalt and Duckfeet's being buried in Capulet's tomb because she took foul poison for love of him. Ha! Except that it wasn't really poison, was it? It was a trick. Your trick. Don't think I've forgotten you married them in secret and then distilled for her that vial of liquor, so that she the semblance of icy death could feign—and then bugger off with him to Mantua. That was a base and shoddy thing to do. They should have *decassocked* you for that. And snipped your rosaries.

Anyway, there's nothing that anyone can wag the thorny finger of reproach at *me* for.

I feel goodly about myself. I really do. Because at the beginning of our marriage I did try. I never mentioned *Her* name once. I even tried to be understanding if he started descanting on Lammas Eve. (That was *Her* birthday, you know. She would have been fourteen at Lammastide, if she'd been able to keep her hands off other people's boyfriends.) The trouble was he wasn't

41

just melancholy at Lammas. It was Lammastide, Candlemas and Martinmas . . . What mass wasn't it! He was three hundred and sixty-five days of the year melancholy! Unnatural creature that he was. That's why I used to let him come and make his ghostly confession to you—anything to get him out of my portals. Except that then you let slip that he spent most of the time decrying me behind my back *but you couldn't divulge a word of it because the confessional was sacred!* You're such a petty, meddlesome fool, aren't you?

'Shrew me though, I'm not saying that things were *always* bad between us. The Prince himself danced at our nuptials and everyone was delighted that Romeo had married the kind of girl who got invited to Capulet parties. I was the peace-maker of Verona, wasn't I? Mind you, I was a morsel put out that Romeo thought he could just pick up with me where he left off. I felt I was entitled to be wooed and sighed over a *bit*, you know, a few *ah me*'s, one or two *alack-a-days* considering how he'd dumped me the first time round. Not that I got any. Nevertheless I will attest, to my dying day, that we were happy and did cavort quite merrily together at first. But, after a while, a woman doth lose her sweet mystery. That's the problem. You find when you get past thirty that people hardly rate your favours at all, not as a woman. Whereas of course with *Her* he'd only had the one night. He hadn't even had time to find out she'd got flat feet.

Sooth, it was the first time he'd ever lain with anyone! Of course he enjoyed it, particularly as Webfoot knew a trick or two. She might have been only thirteen but she'd been around a bit. Oh yes, I bet the last fifteen years up there she's been playing the Elysian Field like no one's business.

But for Romeo, you see, the big problem is I'm not a fond memory, for the dewy-eyed remembrance of, am I? I'm someone he actually has to live with. *'Juliet wouldn't have been nagging on at me for ducats all the time.'* That's the kind of descanting I get. On and on, descanting this, descanting that. Well, Juliet didn't have four children and a palazzo to run! I wish she'd been married to him long enough to find out just how tight-fisted he is. Except when it comes to *teenage girls*, of course!

We did go to Nurse Therapy for a while. To try and put our 'lying together' right. Of course he didn't want to bestir himself for that, and he hated handing over the money, but the Nurse did help me recognise that he has this real problem with *unbosoming* himself. He can't take proximity. He prefers his women distant, unattainable . . . dead, ideally. One good thing did come out of talking it through, however. He had this idea about us 'lying together' on the balcony. It seemed a bit kicky-wicky at first but we both really got into it. Do you know, I really felt we were beginning to achieve a certain genuine *unbosoming*. Then one night he slipped on the ivy and hurt his back quite badly. And do you know what he said? '*This never happened with Juliet!*' The only reason we were doing it on balconies was because they reminded him of Her! Nothing to do with me. I felt anger at that, I really did. And deeply humiliated. *Bosomed* or *unbosomed*, I just wanted him out of my life.

Last week was the final straw. I'd warned him: you can't go sniffing around thirteen-year-old girls and hope to get away with it forever. I *knew* one day he'd get caught. She was only two years older than my eldest! You probably haven't heard. The Prince is trying to keep the whole business dark within the closet of his counsel because the girl is old Martino's daughter and he's a Capulet. The last thing anyone wants is the Caps getting all stirred up against the Montagues again. They haven't forgiven him for Tybalt, or County Paris, or little Webfoot for that matter. So I went to see the Prince myself, did you know that? No, of course you wouldn't, would you? I asked him if there was any manner in which we might 'scape the public shame for my household, the retribution against my children and the eruption of civil brawling once Romeo went to trial.

'Not easy,' he said. 'You know what our Rebellious Subjects are like. Anything for a brawl.'

'But what if Romeo were suddenly to die in prison?' I asked.

'Alas the day,' replied the Prince. 'The gaolers will have taken from him anything that might aid a man in the desperate act of taking his own life. Even unto his hose.'

'Ah, but what if he were to drink a vial of poison, so cunning and so rapid that it leaveth no trace at all, naught but the cold hand of icy death?' I asked. 'You know the kind of thing.'

'Alack, who might have the wit to smuggle such a poison unto him?' the Prince enquired of me.

'Why,' said I. 'Why, his dearly beloved *wife*, she might. What if she were to bring him food and softest mead that just happened to be laced with such a poison, all the while dissembling that she were providing her poor lord with succour during the lonely watch of his imprisonment?'

'Well,' said the Prince, 'we should say that such a woman would have done the state a great service in the prevention of civil brawls, and pernicious rage, of the kind that our Rebellious Subjects do having a liking for. Moreover we should extend our protection in her grievous widowhood, should it prove necessary— which, by the way, we very much doubt.'

So, father. I have come hither today to ask you to forgive me for I have sinned mortally. About ten minutes ago in fact. May I, however, remind you of the silent sanctity of this confessional. If a word of this gets out I'm sure the Prince will make sure something pretty nasty happens to your canticles. Oh, and don't rush round there with an antidote this time, please. The Palace has provided me with something a little stronger than your usual.

Don't look so downcast. Think of Romeo. At last he will be reunited with his Juliet. Personally I am delighted for them both. I just hope she likes them middle-aged, mean and fat.

As for me, I've told the Prince I'm usually on my balcony around nine o'clock most evenings . . .

Whatever Happened To . . .
THE ARTFUL DODGER?

Mr Dawkins stood and surveyed his ships with the satis-
faction of a man who has seen great deeds done in his
name and great empires built upon it. Like Alexander
he had conquered a vast part of the known world but
unlike Alexander Mr Dawkins did not weep, neither
did he, like a true Alexander, show any signs of dying
young and greatly lamented, for Mr Dawkins had lived
already into a prosperous middle age. In truth Mr
Dawkins' time for dying young and lamented had long
since passed. It was many years since the spires of Her
Majesty's Penitentiary had loomed so darkly over the
young apprentice Dawkins, and much muddy water
had flowed past his alma mater since Mr Dawkins had
graduated, ten years later, a veritable *baccalaureus* in
villainy.

Indeed, had it not been for a very lucrative trade
presenting itself to Mr Dawkins as soon as Her Majesty
had completed taking her pleasure of him, there is no
doubt that he would have put his freshman years to
excellent effect. Fortune it therefore was that thrust a
cargo of dubious publications under our young gradu-

ate's nose and told him that he might sell them to lonely gentlemen bound for a career in the colonies. Fortune was generous to Mr Dawkins that day, Fortune, or rather the small pornographer whom Mr Dawkins was at that time robbing with excessive violence. For the sale of these disreputable lithographs formed the basis of our gentleman's subsequent wealth and rise to respectability. In the months that followed Mr Dawkins' Personal Export Service shipped out hundreds of illustrations of poor, but generous-hearted, young women who seemed unable to afford sufficient underwear.

Such was the enthusiasm that greeted the sale of these heartrending images in the charitable colonies that Mr Dawkins soon began shipping out the young women as well. These rosy-cheeked and copper-haired females were scholars of an enquiring mind whose greatest desire was to see the parts of far-flung empire, and also the parts of those who served within those parts. Mr Dawkins' remarkable business acumen proved to be a university of life that enabled men and women of all stations to gain a knowledge of the world, and of each other. In return Jack Dawkins' distinguished alumni repaid their tutor handsomely.

But these days Mr 'Jackdaw' Dawkins, Mr Artful Dodger as once he was known, took little interest in the educational wing of his soaraway enterprise. Two professors of urban economics, Mr Knuckles and Mr Kneecap Charley, ran the export/import trade for their celebrated vice-chancellor whilst he devoted himself to spreading the benefits of vice to higher places. Over the years Mr Dawkins had come to own many beautiful and exotic objects but what he most wished to acquire was his very own member of parliament and to this end he was generosity itself in lending money to junior government ministers and arranging for them to make friends with young students of the body politic. Everyone said that it was only a matter of time before Her Majesty eased Mr Dawkins of that tiresome prefix to his surname and replaced it with a much more comfortable knighthood.

Yet today our great Alexander was aware that a something haunted him, not just a something but a figure, and one that had been for some fifteen minutes dogging his every step on the quayside, a figure like unto the shadow of death that had stalked so close behind great Alexander, and yet not like a shadow either for a shadow does not stumble as it darts behind a crate of heavy-duty prophylactics bound for Mandalay, neither does a shadow curse when it trips on a capstan, nor cry out in pain when it lands upon its spectral nose.

'Are you alooking to speak to me?' said Mr Dawkins, addressing the crate and tapping it with his silver-topped cane. 'Out wiv you, man, for I have business to attend to and I will be wery loath to waste my time on the likes of you.'

The shadow stood up and as it did it scraped the

ordure that had attached to its ghostly shoes on to some-thing more substantial.

'Dodger?' it said. 'Am I addressing Mr Jackdaw Daw-kins, once the Artful Dodger of Fagin's gang?'

'I'm not awares of such a name,' replied Mr Dawkins. 'Not aware of any artfuls nor no dodgers, for that matter, but you are addwessing Mr Dawkins who is in the business of owning the wery quayside upon which you are standing, my good man.'

'Mr "Dodger" Dawkins whose ships these be?' asked the spectral figure and, as he gestured, Mr Dawkins saw that this apparition was a thin and ragged one, and as much a stranger to soap as food.

'The wery same,' said Dodger.

'Mr "Dodger" Dawkins whose ships take poor dis-tressed girls to a life of carnal servitude in the East and then return stacked with opium, tantric sculptures and various other articles of a highly dubious nature? Mr "Dodger" who provides generous loans to members of a certain political party?'

'The same,' said Dodger, advancing on the wraith. "If it is any of your business, my fwiend. But who might you be? Speak or shall I simply have you evictated from my quayside.'

'Save your anger, Dodger,' declared the retreating figure. 'For 'tis I, Oliver.'

'Oliver?' repeated Dodger. 'My Oliver weduced to this? Oliver who was my closest, dearwest friend,

the boon companion of my days in penal servitide?'

'No,' replied the ashen spirit. 'The other one.'

'Oh, Oliver the Prat,' said Mr Dawkins.

'He indeed.'

'And what do you want with my time?' asked Dodger, determined to leave behind the memory of a measly, puking child who, thirty years previous, had ratted on Fagin's gang and then got himself adopted by a gullible middle-class philanthropist. The figure approached closer and as it did Mr Dawkins could easily discern that it was well acquainted with sleeping in the doorways of this city and being urinated upon by gentlemen revellers of the night.

'I wish for something, Jack Dawkins,' he explained as the Dodger averted his nose. 'For old times' sake.'

'If it is women you is awanting—' Dodger began, but the grey-faced spectre silenced him with ironic laughter.

'Women! Women cannot help me! Do you not see that I have flowing in my veins the foul degeneracy that caused the downfall of all my family? Women are no use to me.'

'Tantwic exotica, then?' Mr Dawkins suggested. 'We import a most efficacious line from Bombay.'

'Hear me, Dodger,' the ghost interrupted. 'Hear me. Those of us who have reached the bottommost rung of human depravity still need to ease our pain until the day when death releases us from the depravity of our life.'

53

'Bar of soap?'

Oliver gripped the Dodger's shoulder in his bony hand. 'Money. I need money, Dodger, to feed the foul addictions to which my poor degenerate body is prey.'

'How much?' asked Mr Dawkins who wished to quit this interview, or at least stand upwind of his spectral interlocutor.

'Enough to keep me in laudanum for a month.'

The Dodger would have whistled, for he knew how much he could make from that much opiate just in the Palace of Westminster, but before his lips could issue forth a single sibilation a second calculation formed within his troubled mind.

'And *after* that month?'

'Then I will come and visit you again, Mr Dawkins. Fear not, my depravity has made me shameless.'

Our Alexander furrowed his brow. He was beyond whistling now and could not have pursed his lips to save the life of Jackdaw Dawkins, let alone that of the fabled and irrelevant King of Macedonia.

'And lest your conscience thinks better of encouraging the dread addiction from which I suffer,' Oliver hissed, 'I have armed myself with this.'

Mr Dawkins was at that moment about to cry *alarum*, in all directions, for he expected the rancorous demon to draw a firearm from inside its rags, but instead Oliver merely produced an envelope.

'This letter fell into my hands by a route that need be of no concern. It may surprise you to learn that I still have friends from a more noble walk of life and, whilst abusing their hospitality recently, I discovered that some of them, members of Her Majesty's Opposition all, I believe, have written to Mr Gladstone enclosing proof that one J. Dawkins, Esquire of the City of London is bribing members of the government. Moreover, they demand that Mr Dawkins' very good friend the Attorney General is instructed to prosecute this hypocritical villain forthwith.'

At this moment Dodger made a lunge to seize the missive from its current owner, but Oliver had not forgotten how Fagin had schooled him in dodging and weaving. Quickly the wraith sidestepped his opponent.

'Now, J. Dawkins, Esquire,' said Oliver. 'What say you and I inspect the good ship *Nancy* where I'm told you store the exotic statuary that your agents hack down from Indian temples—and where I hear you have discovered a novel and intriguing place to secrete your petty cash? I have a great desire to forward this letter to the Houses of Parliament and am only likely to forget my purpose if you open up your coffers.'

'But the letter?' said Dodger.

'This is my insurance,' Oliver replied, folding it up inside his pocket. 'For I mean to have a guaranteed income from you, Dodger.'

'Well,' said Mr Dawkins, swallowing hard and

making way for Oliver to pass up the gangplank. 'Let us go on board, then. You know Oliver, my dear . . . it's been too long, we must be better acquainted in the future.'

'I'm sure we shall be,' said Oliver, and so intent was he upon his booty that he little noticed how the Dodger's arm circled his waist in a show of affection.

'Old Fagin would be pleased to see how you've wemembered all he taught you in our gweener days,' said Mr Dawkins.

'You were never green,' Oliver replied as they reached the deck. 'But now you've grown into a mighty oak, Dodger, I intend to cling to you like ivy. You will be my support and my sustenance in the years to come.'

Yet at that very moment the mighty oak seemed to stumble and in stumbling it took a grip upon the ivy and forced it over the gunwales and into the murky depths of St Katherine's Dock.

'Why, I do weckon we have a man overboard,' said Dodger to Mr Kneecap Charley who had appeared quickly on deck. 'And a poor wetch at that. Charley, my dear, do wun and tell the authowities, I believe there is a watchman in Gwavesend who deals with such misfortunes.'

Thus saying, Mr Dawkins returned to the quayside, for he had business that day with a charitable trust he was setting up under the aegis of Mr Gladstone, and a statue of particular significance to deliver to the Archbishop of Canterbury's private garden. As he passed over the spluttering, half-submerged figure of Oliver Brownlow Mr Dawkins looked down and patted the pocket of his tailcoat wherein now lay the envelope that had so briefly been in his friend's possession.

Oliver was not the only one who had well remembered all that Fagin taught.

Whatever Happened To . . .
DOROTHY?

Little Hope Farm,
Moosegender,
Kansas 90516.

Dear Jemimah-Lou Horsebaum,

I thank you for your letter enquiring after what happened to me when I returned from the Land of Oz, full sixty year ago. I have to say that I had not realised my notoriety had spread as far as Hogsnappet Springs, Missouri.

For several days, Jemimah-Lou, I looked at your letter where it rested on the mantel in my parlour and I wondered whether I should reply to you at all, but finally your pappy's words persuaded me. Your father, who is a good man I trust, described you as an 'imaginative young girl'. Those words worry me greatly, Jemimah-Lou, they leave me sufficiently afeared for you that I have decided, after all, that I should tell my terrible tale once more.

I was brought up the American way: we feared God

in our family, told the truth and always carried a shot-gun. Three months after I was born my own pappy was killed in a duel with a crackshot bible salesman and my mother, for failing to observe the seventeen months of mourning laid down by Ezekiel, was driven out of town, tarred and lynched.

But the years that followed were blissfully happy ones for me. I lived with my Aunt Em and Uncle Henry in our simple one-room home on the prairie. Ours was a quiet god-fearing household where nothing much ever happened except, of course, that one day a freak cyclone blew across Kansas and swept our house up into the clouds with me and my dog, Toto, inside it.

I was gone from United States territory for a total of twenty-seven days, Jemimah-Lou. And when I returned I soon found myself a scandal as, I assume, you must be aware from all the newspaper reports. I have to say that my problem was—and is still—that I'm too goldurned honest for my own good. Aunt Em she comes out of the new house my uncle had just finished building, right there where the old one had been, and she says to me, 'My darling child! Where in the world have you come from?' *And what did I say?* I should have made up some hocum like I'd been living with the Injun, or flat on my back in a Wichita bordello, but no, I stood there, four-square on my two little feet, and told them the truth. 'Oh, from the Land of Oz, Aunt Em,' says I.

Damn me for the fool I was, didn't I tell my foster-parents every durn thing that had happened? How I had come down slap on top of the Wicked Witch of the East and killed her flat. How I had had many wonderful adventures with a scarecrow, a lion and some retard who walked around in a suit of tin cans. And how I met with this useless horse doctor of a wizard before Glinda, the Good Witch of the South, told me that if I clicked together my silver shoes they would take me anywhere in the world that I wanted to go, even back to Kansas.

'And did you have any silver shoes with you, child?' my uncle asked.

'Why yes, Uncle,' said I. 'I had with me the silver shoes that had belonged to the Wicked Witch of the East.'

'This is the lady you killed?' asked my aunt.

'Yes indeedy, Aunt Em,' says I. 'Her shoes were all that remained when I had squashed her flat and they were presented unto me by the Munchkin people who were rejoicing that I had brought to an end the Wicked Witch's tyranny.'

'Is that so?' said my uncle, clearing his throat and backing towards the door.

'But child, child!' said my aunt. 'Are you really telling me that you were responsible for the death of this poor east coast lady, and that you then stole from her corpse?'

That night I heard my aunt and uncle conferring and whispering together while I lay in my bed but I was just about as pleased as blueberry pie to be back home with Toto and so I did not attend when I heard them speak of 'what should be done with Dorothy'. The next morning, however, after prayers had been said and the Lord roundly praised for all his excellent goodness, my aunt explained to me that they were not entirely sure if they could believe my curious account.

'It *is* a remarkable story,' I agreed, hugging her.

'So, child, what your uncle and I have decided is that he will thrash you with his belt, to see if that will bring you to your senses.'

After Uncle Henry had finished whupping me I still held to my story, although my hide was by then red and raw. I was sent upstairs with some of Ichabod's patent soothing ointment while my uncle and aunt discussed what they should do next. My uncle was all for turning me over to the county sheriff, in case he had received reports of any ladies squashed flat and robbed of their footwear within the past four weeks, but my aunt, who was a god-fearing woman and a sight bigger than my uncle, prevailed in her view that I should be taken to the Reverend Roberts.

I have to tell you, Jemimah-Lou, that while I was in the land of Oz I was kidnapped, enslaved, threatened with physical violence (by all manner of strange mutants) squashed by the Quadlings and nearly drugged to death in a field of magic poppies, but all this was nothing to what happened to me next.

The Reverend Obadiah Roberts was a vain and foolish man who believed in the numbing power of prayer, the cleansing properties of water and the shocking effects of electricity. When I told him the story of my adventures in the Land of Oz he declared that either I was a lying little hussy or I had been cavorting with the devil who had filled my pretty little head with dangerous nonsense. Either way I was plumb certain to be in need of correction. The following Sunday, therefore, I was duly prayed over before being immersed in a tin bath of consecrated water and my finger stuck into a light socket. This was pretty plumb well normal when the Church of Divine Illumination undertook the correction of imaginative teenage girls.

Despite the severe pain that I endured that Sunday morning I continued to hold out that I had been to Oz and travelled down the Yellow Brick Road, for this was indeed God's truth. After the service several women of the church kindly helped apply bandages. They then lined up outside the church to spit and denounce me for a brazen Jezebel and strumpet.

Please understand my uncle and aunt were compassionate people. It did distress them greatly to see me endure so much pain and they were right sorry that I had to walk back to our little prairie house all by myself. As a kindness they actually followed close behind in the

pony and trap, just in case I should stumble and fall.

When I arrived home Lukas Hornswoggler was standing on our porch.

'Miss Dorothy,' he said. 'I have come for to visit you because we have had an understanding for many years now that as soon as you was legal we would be agettin' hitched.'

'That is so, Lukas,' I replied.

'Well now, Miss Dorothy. Now that my mommy tells me you are an accursed concubine of the great Satan, and a lying strumpet to boot, I am just calling by to say it doesn't look likely we can have an understanding anymore. D'you understand me?'

'Indeed I do, Lukas,' I replied.

'In which case I will say good-day to you then, ma'am,' he said, tipping his hat. 'I'm right sorry to have bothered you.'

The following week I was taken back to church again, and the week after that. I have to admit that it did occur to me, while the congregation were crying hosanna over my immersions and electrocutions, that I could henceforth always *lie* unto my aunt and uncle and the Reverend Roberts. Henceforth I could declare that it had all been a dream and thereby spare myself from further torture. But alas, my upbringing had not schooled me in such deceit and so instead I suffered and prayed to the Lord when I could keep my thoughts straight.

I am glad to say that the Good Lord did look mercifully upon my misfortunes, because in the fourth week of my ordeal 'Old Redemption', the Reverend Roberts' generator, blew up. As the congregation rushed outside to smother the flames, I detached myself from the electrical apparatus and wandered into the bright sunlight. Through the smoke and fumes I saw the strangest sight. For a moment it seemed as if the Scarecrow, my old friend from the Yellow Brick Road, had come to testify to the truthfulness of what I said, for there he stood at the corner of Ticklemoser's field, his arms outstretched to embrace me. Although my legs were still very weak, I ran as best I could and threw my arms around him. 'Oh Scarecrow,' I cried. 'Have you come to save me? Have you brought my silver shoes so I can click them together and escape from this terrible place?'

People had stopped dousing the flames and were now looking up at me.

'Look!' I cried. 'It's Scarecrow. He's come to tell you it's all true. Every word I said to you. Any minute now the Tin Man and Lion will be here and the Good Witch of the South!'

The congregation now gaped at me, open-mouthed. Then it was that I realised this was just Ticklemoser's old scarecrow, the one that Lukas and his friends used to dress in ladies' bloomers and do strange things to every fourth of July, but it was too late. Half the congregation wanted to see me burned for talking of witches—

65

and the other half for talking of the South: they still hated Louisiana. My uncle and aunt seized me, bundled me away as quickly as they could and brought me to the Lonesome Sanitarium for my own safety.

And that, Jemimah-Lou, is how I came to spend the rest of my youth in the county sanitarium. After a year or so the doctors realised that I was not mad at all but I was told that there was no place for me at Little Hope Farm now because my aunt had been unable to find anyone in the whole state of Kansas who was much interested in my marriage prospects, given the disgrace I had brought upon our family. So I remained at Lonesome until my aunt and uncle died and I inherited this farmstead.

I have now been here on my own for more than thirty years, Jemimah-Lou, and I have to tell you that Oz was a bad thing to happen to anyone. You must not blame me for being a bitter and twisted old woman. I am glad to read that you believe in the Scarecrow, the Tin Man and Lion, and so you should for I have always told the truth—much good has it done me. As for what happened to me after I returned from Oz . . . well here in this letter, Jemimah-Lou, I have today put down the truth. You can choose to believe me—or you can go fry your head.

Dorothy Luftschaffter (Miss)

Whatever Happened To . . .
JIM HAWKINS?

Full many a year it is since the squire and Dr Livesey fought their famous duel. ' 'Tis but a fleshwound, Livesey,' said the squire, with good heart, before he contracted pneumonia waiting for the surgeons to arrive, and so died.

The cause of the bitter enmity between the squire and the doctor was our Great Disappointment on discovering that the treasure we brought back to Bristol was, to the last doubloon, base metal counterfeit and entirely worthless. Old Ben Gunn was the only one to be neither surprised nor distressed. 'I allus did wonder why the Cap'n of the old *Jolly Blagger* put up no fight,' he cackled.

'But surely you must have had some *other* treasure on board!' the doctor shouted, dashing the wedge of Double Gloucester from Ben's hand.

'Ah, that we did,' said Ben. 'And I'll wager all that was in the bag Long John Silver took with him when he jumped ship in old Barbadee.'

Each man took the Great Disappointment according to his own nature. Old Ben little cared what fortune he owned as long as he could beg enough coin to satisfy his dairy product addiction, but the doctor and Squire Trelawney blamed each other roundly. 'Dammee, man!' cried the squire. 'You're the one with an education. You should have been able to tell what was gold and what *pyrite*! The Trelawneys have never been up to that kind o'thing but I'll wager ye could have told, had ye not been chasing young Jim around the ship from morn till midnight.'

'Oh, mother, what shall we do?' said I, for after Squire Trelawney's death Mr Blandly, and the other gentlemen who had stood bail for our expedition, took possession of his estate and boarded everything up so there was no work and no money left in the village.

'Do?' cried my mother, surveying the empty tables in the 'Admiral Benbow' inn, but she found no answer to her own question other than to kick me roundly before breaking into sobs.

'You have been halfway round the world with that brainless squire and so-called doctor and this is all you bring back!' she cried, God rest her soul, and then she fell greatly unto the bottle. Three weeks later, having fulsomely abused all men and consumed everything that could be drunk within the inn, my mother died of what Dr Livesey called a surfeit but what I will maintain to this day was a broken heart.

'Ah, ye be an orphan now, Jim lad,' said Old Ben Gunn who had lost none of his wondrous skill at stating the obvious. 'What will ye do with the "Admiral Benbow" inn, Jim? Will ye sell it and set yourself up in a nice little dairy somewhere, making curds and whey, butter pats and junket, eh? What say you, Jim?' and he started to jump up and down with glee.

'No, Ben,' said I. 'I will do my duty by the good people who rely upon the "Admiral". Though I be but a callow youth I will take over the running of this hostelry myself.'

'But, Jim!' cried Ben. 'There is nothing here to drink, your good mother—God rest her thirsty soul—having consumed all that could be poured into a pint pot and swallowed. There is not even the merest morsel of cheese. Believe me, I've checked.'

'Ben, we will be partners in this venture,' said I, for I had developed a fondness for bold but foolish gestures. 'Ben, though your wits be gone, we are all who are left and we must work together.' And so we did. And thus it fell out that within a year I had lost every scrap of money that remained to me, every piece of furniture and every chattel, with the exception of a three-legged four-poster bed and one sea-chest of my mother's old clothes which the bailiff had refused to take because it still reeked of brandy.

'Oh, Jim, now ye be in a worse state than before,' said Ben, but he was not overly distressed, for my last true friend had recently found himself a position as assistant gillikin splugger to the diocesan rat-catcher and was busy appropriating cheese from the bishop's mouse-traps. 'Ah, fear not, Jim lad!' cried he, seeing me greatly cast down. 'You trust old Ben, for we shall hang lights out upon the marsh at nightfall and travellers will think 'tis the fiends making to bear them off and so afeared will they be, poor souls, that they will seek a bed at the inn and order themselves a nice cheese supper which will make your fortune, hee hee!'

'I doubt this plan, Ben,' said I, 'but as I have forsworn all alcohol I believe there is no option left open to me.'

And so it was, and so indeed did we make a little money, enough to get by, from the one bed that was remaining and the cheese that Ben could prise from the jaws of his decapitated rats. Until, that is, one cold wet night when good old Ben was out fixing lanterns in the marsh and sank into the peatbog without trace. Left upon my own again, and pretty much as cast down as one can be, I might easily have followed my mother to the grave had I not signed the pledge, and had there actually been something to drink within the 'Admiral Benbow' inn.

One dark night some months later, I heard a rapping upon the door and, to my surprise, found Dr Livesey who had returned from London where he had been living in Soho with a soldier of fortune. I had not seen the doctor since my mother's death but still I took the precaution of never bending over in front of him, just as I had on our voyage to Treasure Island. The doctor had forever been inviting me to walk arm in arm with him round the deck, or sending me to warm his berth before he retired for the night, and indeed my mother had warned me before I embarked on the *Hispaniola* that she suspected something mighty queer about Dr Livesey. 'Jim,' she said, 'the squire cares only for money to cover his debts. That I can understand. But the doctor has a goodly income from the sick folk of this parish. His only interest seems to be that you should ship with them as cabin boy. I am afeared and would not let you go were it not for this large sum of money they have paid me to release you from your duties here.' But even had my mother's words not been ringing in my ears I should have been put on my guard by the good-hearted seadogs whom I used to hear complaining of the doctor's evening visits to check for scurvy, and other ailments of the privy parts.

'Ahoy there, Jim!' cried the doctor as he stood in the doorway. 'Any chance of shivering me timbers tonight?'

In our village the doctor had always dressed in sombre black and been a bachelor of conspicuous rectitide, but once we left Bristol he had begun to disport himself about the deck with uncommon extravagance and to clap me on the shoulder whenever he passed. Often I would only escape his attentions by hiding in the *Hispaniola*'s apple barrel.

On our return voyage, with the crew depleted by death and desertion, he became even more intent on me. Often he would wink in a most ungentlemanly fashion and, after a tot or two of rum, would throw off his wig and insist on being called 'Dr Lovesey'. Indeed, Mr Silver's last words to me, before he jumped ship in Barbados, were, 'Mind how ye go, Jim lad, and watch out for the doctor. He's one for the old Jolly Roger if ever I saw 'un.'

When we were first back in England the doctor once again disported himself like a pillar of sober rectitide, particularly while he and the squire were abusing each other, but now he was returned from London I noticed he had that old seadog look in his eye again. 'Woof, woof!' he cried. 'And how about a game of David and Jonathan, Jim lad? For I see the inn is empty tonight.'

'The inn is empty most nights,' I replied, offering him a seat from where I stood against the wainscot, but the doctor was not to be gainsaid. He clapped me in his arms and exclaimed, 'Oh Jim, oh Jim, my fine boy! I have such a taste for the sea, you know.'

'It's just over the cliff, Dr Livesey,' said I. 'You can't miss it.'

'But what about a touch of yo-ho-ho?' he replied.

'We're right out of it,' I explained.

I managed to resist the good doctor's overtures at first, but he returned frequently and on one occasion, having drunk more than was common, even for a member of his calling, he asked for a room and offered to pay handsomely if I would warm his berth for him as I was wont on the old *Hispaniola*. My coffers were so empty that I did as he bade, and more. I even let him dress up in the stays and fol-de-rols that he found among the clothes in my mother's chest. You may imagine my distress when I relate that the next morn I found the doctor had departed before first light and left me scarce enough coin to cover the cost of his food and drink. Three weeks later, however, a banknote for a large sum of money was delivered to me at the inn. There was no letter attending it, and a month later another banknote arrived the same day as the doctor visited me again. Over the next five years these sums of money continued to visit me almost as frequently as the doctor himself, but rarely on the same day. Neither he nor I spoke of the money, although on many a dark night we would splice the mainbrace together, if there were no other customers at the 'Admiral Benbow' inn. I did not welcome the doctor's visits, but they did buffer me against bankruptcy and keep a roof over my head.

And now to bring my sorry tale to its close. Last week great news was brought that the hall was to be let. Everyone rejoiced that prosperity might return again to our small hamlet. I had just finished polishing up the second-best spittoons when there came an unfamiliar rapping on the door. It was not the doctor's cane which always beat out a merry hornpipe, nor was it the familiar truncheon of His Majesty's Customs officers who

occasionally called by when on the trail of some notorious cheese smuggler. No, instead when I opened it was to a fine gentleman in splendid waistcoat and stock, with a gold chain and two ladies hanging on his arm. I would not have known him until he spoke, had it not been for my attention being drawn to the rich and ornately carved pegleg that stood where once there had been no leg at all.

'Jim lad!' cried the man. 'Do you not recognise me, Jim?'

'John Silver?' I asked.

'*Sir* John Silver, MP,' he replied. 'For I have invested my share well, Jim. I had hoped ye would have done more with the money than this, but let us in, Jim, let us in! Lady Silver and her sister are not dressed for the country and there is little in the way of warmth at that old hall of yourn.'

I was pleased to see the old ship's cook looking so prosperous, and delighted to discover that he was to be our new squire. Finding a small measure of rum to give my visitors, I explained that the coin we had carried back to Bristol had proved to be fool's gold.

'Why, Jim, I knew that,' Silver cackled. 'Why else d'ye think I took only one bag when I quitted the *Hispaniola*? I counted out that bag carefully afore we left the island, Jim lad. But I had a conscience, Jim, ye can't say I didn't have a conscience towards ye.'

'You did indeed give me good advice,' I admitted,

wishing I could tell my visitor that I had always heeded it.

'Advice? Nay, not that!' Silver cried. 'I mean the banknotes that I sent you. I felt I owed ye, Jim, as the only honest person on that ship. An hundred pounds I sent across the years. D'ye mean to say you never received the money?'

'Oh yes, indeed I did,' I replied, my head swimming in confusion.

'And ye never guessed it was old John?' the pirate laughed. 'Now who else would be giving you an hundred pounds just like that, Jim Hawkins, eh?'

'Who indeed?' I replied, and I began to feel in need of a drink myself.

Whatever Happened To . . .
SNOW WHITE?

END OF THE FAIRYTALE ROMANCE

It was the wedding of the century. Once upon a time the whole kingdom was in love with the royal couple, and yet within a year the fairytale has turned to dust. The Republican*'s award-winning 'Probe' team looks at the media's role in the disintegration of Snow White's ill-fated marriage*

It was on the royal honeymoon that 'Snowy fever' gripped the Magic Kingdom. Everywhere the royal pair travelled, reporters jostled for photographs of the young bride, leaving the Handsome Prince all but ignored.

Seasoned royal–watcher Gilbert Hangeur-Orne was one of the first to recognise the tell-tale signs of royal displeasure.

'Of course the tabloids much preferred the sensational elements of this story over the fact that the succession would be secured. What everyone wanted to know was what it was like lying in a glass coffin for so many years, how it felt to be restored to life by a single kiss, &c. I remember one reporter asking Snowy what she thought about, all those years she was lying on Lonely Mountain.

"*Oh, I suppose I used to imagine one day my prince will come,*" she replied with a winning smile.

That photo, that smile and that story were flashed all round the world, making Princess Snow an international star overnight. In my mind there was no doubt that the Handsome Prince hadn't expected this. He was used to being cheered and photographed every time he went out rescuing damsels. I think he felt massively excluded.'

Within a few months rumours began to circulate about the unsuitability of the princess for royal life. This newspaper was frequently briefed by an anonymous upper-class caller who described himself as '*Sources close to the Palace*'. He was the first to disclose that doubts were being expressed at a senior level about the prince's choice of wife. Courtiers were said to find her too good to be true, but it was also noted that she never attended when the prince was on his official dragon-slaying engagements. The caller, who refused to be identified, was at pains to point out that no one blamed the prince for his mistake. 'After all, he had hardly known Princess Snow at the time of their betrothal. In fact HRH had only kissed the girl once before they married, and that was in order to bring her back to life.'

There is no doubt that public pressure had been a factor in the prince's hasty marriage. A middle-aged, unmarried heir to the throne was seen as a political liability, and by many as morally dubious. The constitutional historian, James Munnifer Auld-Rope, believes the prince was under pressure from the Wicked Queen to ensure the succession but that, having finally found a virgin to marry, he began privately to regret his actions.

Most newspapers were still besotted with Snowy, however, and few took any notice of the Palace rumour machine. Only *The Republican* gave credence to stories of marital discord and we were censured by the Press Council for doing so.

Finding his tactics unsuccessful, '*Sources close to the Palace*' began trying to discredit the princess directly. Innuendo was used to suggest that, prior to her marriage, the princess had cohabited with a number of men, possibly as many as seven.

At the time of the wedding much had been made of the princess's virginity. The Campaign for Moral Rearmament even advocated that *all* teenage girls eat poison apples and spend a few years in a glass-topped coffin 'so that they may bring to matrimony that innocence which is all too often lacking these days'. This newspaper remained sceptical about the rumours. Previously, whenever the prince had hacked his way into an enchanted castle in search of a bride, the press had made great play of unearthing her sordid sexual past to ensure this particular damsel was ruled out of the running. It was most unlikely they would have missed such a story about Princess Snow. Nevertheless, tabloid journalists the length and breadth of the country went into an orgy of excitement over this lead. While an

unhappy-looking princess fulfilled her regular engagements of being photographed and cheered at, journalists
exhausted their expenses looking for her former lovers.

Initially they drew a blank, and when they door-
stepped the princess herself she would do nothing but
smile and wave as she always did. With the possibility
of the story going cold, '*Sources*' issued a fresh tip-off
that these seven cohabitees were all miners. The tabloid
press repeated this allegation verbatim and whipped
themselves up into a frenzy of indignation. The more
conservative papers were exercised over the possibility
that Princess Snow had been 'slumming it' with
members of the National Union of Mineworkers, while
one editor, notorious for his bad spelling, concocted a
headline that Princess Snowy had been indulging in
underage sex.

After a month of besieging every colliery in the kingdom the story was once again growing cold when police
arrested seven dwarves who were found hiding on top
of Lonely Mountain. These former diamond excavators
had been evicted from the company cottage they rented,
very much at the time that the rumours about Princess
Snow began to circulate. An unidentified royal official
had closed their mine and given them a large sum of
money on condition that they travel away for a year
and a day. Dwarves being notoriously spendthrift, the
money had soon run out and they had returned to
Lonely Mountain, stealing cans of food from a local

supermarket in order to survive. Although the seven miners made no mention of Princess Snow in their statement to police, the fact that they were seven in number, linked to their claim that 'some royal toff paid us to keep our little mouths shut', sent the press into a lather of speculation. **Dwarfgate** was a big story in which excited leader-writers struggled to outdo each other with headlines like: '*Princess Snowy in Kinky Seven-in-a-Bed Romp*', '*Do Little Men Make Better Lovers?*' and '*Do Dwarves come up to size in the Bedroom?*'

It was the sentencing of the seven dwarves to six months in prison for contempt of court that finally turned an ambivalent press against Snowy. The tabloids condemned their heroine for not coming to the rescue of her silent friends. At this point the Wicked Queen herself issued a press statement insisting, '*The prince and princess are extremely happily married, always have been, and will be ever after*', which is familiar royalspeak for terminal marital disharmony.

After the Queen's statement the Princess continued to wave at the cameras on a daily basis, but she was rarely observed to smile. However, a woman with a lisp, claiming to be '*Fwiends of the princess*', did contact several newspapers and express concern that Princess Snow's side of the story should be put. The dwarves were just good friends, it was explained, and her relationship to them was mainly that of chalet maid. It had not been Princess Snow, but a well-meaning and misguided friend of hers, who had paid the dwarves to travel away for a year and a day. Although she was very sorry for her former friends, the Princess's constitutional position had barred her from interfering in the process of law. 'And anyway,' the *Fwiend* added, 'the prince himself isn't all that handsome and he spends most of his time off killing dragons, leaving the poor princess all on her own. As for all those innuendos about the princess's conduct prior to the marriage: I can tell you she was most definitely a virgin before she married the prince, was still a virgin on her wedding day and jolly well still is now!' The caller then concluded in a high-pitched shriek, 'The princess just isn't that kind of girl! And anyway, the prince was never really interested.'

A week later news broke about the total, acrimonious, and irretrievable breakdown of the royal marriage. The Wicked Queen and the prime minister have since been in renewed discussions about finding a suitable damsel to secure the succession. Last night the prince and princess celebrated their wedding anniversary by travelling in separate glass coaches to separate palaces in separate parts of the kingdom.

Whatever Happened To . . .
MAN FRIDAY?

You know what I hate about this *booke* he hath written? It is nothing but lies and I just know what everybody is going to be saying: 'Oh, that Friday, he was *so* fortunate to have been rescued by Massa Crusoe.' Rescued? My fundament. That's what I say. Let me tell you, Friday was not rescued. I was kidnapped.

Not that anyone is going to believeth me.

Don't get me wrong. I'm easy-going sort. I'm willing to agree with most things for a quiet life. I'll say Britannia rules the waves when most of the time their navy is running its stupid self aground—on account of the fact that they have fat-all idea about longitude; I'll even say that daft old Crusoe supported himself alone on a desert island and raised another Eden, if that will help the poor old beardyman earn a groat or two. But to this new idea that I was *rescued* by him . . . what can I say that is printable?

Let me tell ye something of how I came to make the acquaintance of this great fraud, this Robinson Pseudo-Crusoe.

Nobody knew there was a shipwrecked old loon out

84

there on Party Island. Round our lagoon we were quite used to the English smashing up their ships and getting drowned, but somehow this particular old goat had survived and no one knew about it. He'd been there for years, it seems, taking pot-shots at anything that moved and half-starving to death. But most people from my island never went over to Party Island because there was fatty-bum-all to eat and drink there, and no women. Unlike *my* island where a boy cannot move for young nubiles trying to rub cocoanut oil all over him and making out with the mangoes.

But verily I do digress, as they say round here. It was on my eighteenth birthday that my mother gave me my first canoe and me and Matuli decided to paddle over to Party Island. We had to go somewhere because the women back home was getting a bit too frisky with the old nut oil. So we lay on the beach and quaffed a bit, cooked some yams and told a few ribaldries. Then we spotted him, all red in the face, dressed in these ridiculous goatskins and singing awful songs about salvation and mortifying the flesh. Matuli and me could see that the poor old beardy was verily in need of a decent meal, so while his back was turned Matuli slipped some bananas under a cactus and then we did hide ourselves behind a rock. 'God be praised at the fruitfulness of these wondrous bushes!' cried old Crusoe, daft great loon that he was. All the way back to the boats me and Matuli were splitting our sides so much we decided to let some of the boys in on the secret. A week later five of us paddled over—me, Matuli, Okulu and his brothers. There was no sign of the old goat anywhere, but Matuli decided to leave a few footprints in the sand just to see if that might gee him up more than somewhat. We all had a bit of a jocund at that but after half an hour or so I could see that Okulu was getting a bit stroppy on account of the *no showeth*, so I broke out the yams and the best fermented banana juice, and we did live it up in manifold ways.

After putting away a fair amount of fermentation, Okulu wagered me I wouldn't get in the cooking pot and do the Chicken. He was always wagering folk that, but all the boys was gee'd up now and shouting, 'Do the Chicken! Do the Chicken!' and, as it was my party, I felt I had no choice. So I gets in and they all start throwing bread rolls at me and jumping up and down, as one doth, when the next thing I know is this daft old banyan is charging down at us, shooting off little metal balls and hollering 'Cannibals!' The boys they make great speed to the boats, but me I'm stuck in this cooking pot and clambering to get out like a lobster caught in the nets.

'God be praised but I have rescued you,' says the old goat who is scarlet in the face by now and looking like to have a heart attack. 'Thou wilt live with me and I will teach you to fear the Lord and walk in the ways of true virtue.'

Now me, I'm still trying to put my clothes on, while at the same time edging backwards and hoping to get to the canoes, but unfortunately the old goat brings his blunderbuss to bear on me. Now amongst my people there is an ancient wisdom that thou dost not mess with anyone who possesseth the power to pepper thy fundament with nasty bits of metal. So I did some quick obeisance, kissed the ground and set his foot upon my head, &c.

'I will call thee Friday,' says Crusoe, his voice trembling with emotion as he puts a rope around my neck. 'Because that is the day thou wert vouchsafed to me.' (Actually he was ten hours out on account of the time zones but I did not exercise myself to correct his reading of the longitude. What is so great about being called Man Saturday, after all?)

I had hoped that Matuli and the boys would come back to Party Island and rescue me, but clearly word had got around that I was either hanged or full of the little metal bits. My people are practical about that kind of thing. Never one to complain, I set about making life a bit easier for Crusoe and me by ensuring that he ate a balanced diet. As my people are quite medically advanced I was able to nurse him through several illnesses he contracted; I also taught him simple nutritional tricks like the fact that jellyfish taste better cooked and you're only supposed to eat the inside of cocoanuts. Very soon I had mastered his language which was very necessary on account of the fact that he showed no sign of learning mine. Like all Englishmen, the only concession Crusoe made to my native tongue was to speak his own language very loudly and very slowly.

Of course I did plan my escape, but the beardyman kept that rope tight around me and slept with a loaded pistol under his pillow. I was always worried that he'd roll over in his sleep one night and fill both our fundaments with little metal nasties.

As the years went by I have to say that I did grow fond of the old goat, although he never talked of anything but religion and sex—or rather the virtues of abstinence— two subjects which amongst my people are considered to be rather bad form at the dinner-table. Crusoe had this belief that he had been shipwrecked on Party Island for the expiation of his sins and he refused to believe me when I suggested a more rational explanation relating to the inability of his countrymen to navigate in a straight line or even organise a yam-up in a mango swamp.

Still, we lived well enough until one day some more old goats crash their ship on to our island and Crusoe gets their agreement to take him home. This is my chance, I think, and I'm about to shake hands with the old fool and tell him to steer clear of atolls in future when I'm grabbed by the captain of this ship, clapped in leg irons and shoved into the hold.

'Where are you taking me, Massa?' I cry.

'Home, my boy, home!' he replies.

'Oh good,' say I, but I am dubious, especially when the journey takes seven weeks which is a long time to reach an island just over the horizon, even by British standards.

Of course where we fetch up is this *London*, a damnably cold, wet place where the women wear false buttocks to make their fundaments even bigger and the men stand around talking about how cold and wet it is. Soon as we're down that gangplank I suggest to Crusoe that we find ourselves a few cheap women and some food that containeth a trace of vitamins, but he's adamant that I should see the sights, especially London's famous auction rooms. 'Have I told you about how we trade in my country?' he asks as we walk along, making to dodge the large buckets of urine that Crusoe's countrymen liketh to lobb out of their windows. I am just starting to outline some of my reservations about the inherent dangers of a monetary system over barter when we arrive at a well-appointed commercial house in Cheapside.

'What is for sale here?' I ask.

'Why, you, my boy,' says Crusoe and he shakes my hand, bidding me keep my pecker up at all times. Before I have a chance to ask him which part of the human anatomy he is actually referring to, this big hairy baboon sticks a necklace of teeth round my neck and a bone through my hair. When I ask him what the fatty fundament he thinks he's doing the hairy one explaineth that cannibals are selling better this month.

Like I say, I am an easy-going sort, but this time Crusoe have gone too far. I am still telling him where he can stick his stupid pecker when I am bought by an African gentleman called Moses Katanga who tells me he is impressed by my imaginative and expressive usage of the English language. It turns out Moses is in need of an interpreter because he has been trading slaves with the English for some months now but has no idea how to talk to them about the weather which is an integral part of the business etiquette over here.

All of which do almost bring me up to date. I've been working for Mr Katanga for two years now and, apart from the damp, the urine flying through the air and the absurd fat bottoms on these London women, life over here suiteth me. Fortunately Mr K holdeth not with all this religion, abstinence and bad food that the English enjoy, so we get on fine. I've been able to help him with his enterprises by explaining longitudinal variations which have consistently defeated the English, and he has rewarded me for my diligence. Next year I was even hoping to buy my freedom and perchance travel home. Then last week I was invited to an assembly which is being held to mark the publication of a new *booke*. The publishers were very keen that one Friday the Cannibal, Esq. should grace the event with his presence.

Why me? I thought. Ye can guess what cometh next. What is this *booke* that everyone is talking about? What do it say on the card? Verily nothing but *The Life and Strange Surprising Adventures of Robinson Crusoe, Gent., as Related by Himself.* Gent, my fundament! I run round to the printers and ask if I can see an advance copy. So distracted am I that I arrive completely drenched from head to foot, but that indignity is nothing to what I read within! What a total fatty tum-tum fundament of travesty do I find here. Nowhere is there any mention of how *I* keep Crusoe alive all those years. How I keep him sane, how I teach that pineapples taste better if you peel them first. Friday is presented for all posterity as an ignorant savage. This from a man who knew less about navigation than the sheep who shitteth daily over his cactus crops! Here is Friday, who was the prisoner of this daft old fart for so many years, presented as *grateful* for all that he was taught! Here is Friday, Crusoe's boon companion, *rescued* from savagery. Nowhere is there any mention of the Friday who is kidnapped, manacled, sold into slavery and told that everything will be fine as long as he sticks a bone through his hair and keeps his pecker in the air!

Yet what can I do? In this primitive society there is no one to whom a misrepresented member of a racial minority can appeal. My sole recourse is to write my own account and publish it privately which is what I have now resolved to do. The only problem is, amongst my people there is an ancient wisdom that sequels never sell as well.

Be that as it may, I take up my pen now in the year 1719 . . .